Echoes from Africa

The Land We Call Home

Echoes from Africa

The Land We Call Home

Peter E. Bedzrah

EXCELLER BOOKS®
A GLOBAL PRESS

Echoes from Africa
The Land We Call Home

Cover design by Exceller Books

ISBN: 978-93-48892-68-3

First published in India in 2025 by Exceller Books,
An imprint of GE Group
Address: G1, Dream Apartment, Degree College Road, Belgharia,
Kolkata, 700056, India
www.excellerbooks.com

EXCELLER BOOKS®
A GLOBAL PRESS

Dedication

This piece of art is dedicated, with love and sincerity, to orphans and displaced persons around the world.

Acknowledgement

Penmanship, like most talents, demands the collaboration of diverse skills to be refined. To acknowledge people in writing may be a great honour—but in my opinion, it is still an insufficient gesture to truly extend a heartfelt handshake. Nevertheless, I accept the limitations placed on humanity by precedent.

In light of this, I wish to borrow nature's time and space to honor a few crucial individuals—without whose support, your beloved *Echoes from Africa: The Land We Call Home* would not have been published.

As a mortal man who may not outlive more than eight decades, I consider it a privilege to first honor Jehovah God for His guidance and blessings.

I extend heartfelt gratitude to Madam Christine Esi Gadi for her emotional and financial support. She has been a wonderful mother to me.

I am deeply thankful to Mr. Joshua Adzri for lending me both his time and his space.

And finally, even if my pen ever falls into the depths of forgetfulness, it will never fail to remember Madam A. Alberta and Mr. Colins Asempapa for their boundless love and kindness.

To everyone who, in one way or another, supported me in bringing this piece of art to life—gratias tibi.

Contents

The Ballot That Spilled My Blood

When I numbered the ballot that spilled my blast,
And could tell the figure that drank my life;
When I revived the history that held my past,
To know the wrongs that transpired o'er the strife;
When the yards speak myriads laid to rest,
Which issued from guns invented to infest,
And orphans roam the streets in tattered zest,
Scattered from homes which once made them the nest,
Then shrewdity of man do I query,
That our sagacity should in waste be tabled,
For nothing of man ever prevail in goodwill beset
And we strive for vanities so set to disable;
Little would ever man's propensity upset
Take console therefore in pages that bulked the Bible.

The Shepherd That Became the Wolf

When I remember the vices that became his virtues,
And could page the many oaths that today echo in retrospect;
When the lofty poles bow to salute his commands,
And the soldiers' footsteps hour'd the time;
When before my gaze the people stood on stakes—
To his appeasement, these atrocities bespectacled;
When the media, sheepishly, his neck exonerate,
Feeding on the debris of a comradeship duties beset;
When I beheld how the shepherd dog transmogrified into a wolf,
Only for the herd his canines brushed to snow—
Then to philosophy do I turn for a silent refuge.
Our nation has enthroned a Satan, deigned to be.
But speak while your tongue remains yet untrimmed,
For only the silent can, in silence, be silenced.

The Ancient Graveyard

Too many hearses have I heard wail,
Flattering the bodies therein with repugnant cries.
Leading the parade, friends and families came to hail,
Crowding town streets for a lonely departure apprised.
The grave might be a lonely and dark home,
With a thousand gems staked on its visage.
Yet so has it been decreed, ages past,
That each soil beneath a sole be a trace—
Dust of older generations buried before us.
Tread, therefore, gently; someone has been buried there.
The earth is but a great ancient graveyard.
We live as mortals, but once is a cemetery.
Waiting are we to drop into our lonely graves someday.
Kin, be careful where you step; someone has been buried there.

No Execution Tonight

Had I a knight's blade shy but sharp
Concealed beneath my ancient head grey but graced
I would against armies that did thy heart apart match
To the fairest flaming incorporeal I would entrust thee
And myself match to retribute thy lost
My grandsire was great and mighty
His army many enemies' empires did surpassed
To him belonged the most borrowed legions
Of fearsome titans of the old world
Within my mortal coat lives his remains
And I am supposed to transcend him a thousandfold.
But my lady,
Now that civil duty begot my heart so well
To lay me across a land large and vast
And the people's tongues grafted onto mine
Statesmanship require of me
To my wrath a taming do
Like the domesticated oven between your members.
Had I the knight's blade shy but sharp
Concealed beneath my ancient head grey but cray
I would your wish ever execute.

Auctioning the State

Changing lanes,
Dodging traffics,
Cutting shoulders,

I finally arrived!

Today,
I did my part in auctioning my state.
I attended the funeral
Of a certain minister of resources.
In fact, it was rather an auctioning party.

The funeral resonated state resources.
His Wills reflected thefts,
And his codicils terrified my patriotic spirit.
Extravagant state properties were religiously
Bequeathed to family and co.
Then, fuel, minerals and forest reserves
Were reserved for more important guests.

The phrase, all these I legally own
Kept me thinking on my return trip.
I drove my perplexed self,
Back to my old rusted bungalow.
Instead of a private home paid for,
I chose to live here disgracefully.
My wife hummed many times.
Which warranted an inquisition.

To make known her perturbation,
She asked, *Ikem, what of his Will?*

I smiled with a mischievous gesture.
Picking debris of the only meat pie
I took in lieu of lunch.
I replied; *He willed the state to his family.*
Hearing this, she exclaimed;
What are you also hoarding for us?
Which bothered and scared me.
Not knowing the best answer,
I mention to her the unplanned plan,
To celebrate her birthday at a waterfall.
In hope of changing the matter on her lips,
I committed myself rather.

I did a part.
I partook in auctioning the state today.
Insensitive executors did the execution.
And it ripped my patriotic conscience!

When the Rivers Thirst

Mr. Speaker,
When the abundant lacks abundance,
And the rivers thirst in continuum...
When the wet sky puffs out dry clouds,
And the ground responds
With nasolabial crevices.

When trees weep for death of leaves and roots,
And man responds with hunger.
When the oasis expands into steam,
And the desert strife wet throats with thirst.

When the oceans overflow with nothingness,
And aqua life swims woefully on hot soils.
When the land is polythenised,
And the corns on our tables are but plastics.

When the glaciers decompose
Into iced molecules,
And the poles atrophy.
When the winds stall,
And temperatures remain red.

When our duplicates are born without peripherals,
And the mothers spill red dye.
When the military have no sapiens to rain bullets on,
And emissions modify our genes.

When glasses of water become beakers of chlorine,
And the doctor's incumbency we frequent.
When our lungs find no oxygen in the air we breath,

And our age gauge targets and perks at thirty-nine.

When acid rain reciprocates the good,
And our crops witheringly reply.
When we wear plastic internals
As a result of diuturnal chemical ulcerations,
And our lifespan is catalogued and shelved.

It is then that you will know,
How dearly,
How weighty,
How urgent,
How consequential issues of Climate Change are.
Let us have the Climate Change Action Bill
On the floor right now for its passage,
Mr. Speaker!

Homeless

Caking skin
Burning hair
Tentful possessions.

He's a number one outsider.
He lives on Capitol road
Of the capital city of the world's Capital.
What a spectacle to the United Nations!

Winter feeds on his skin
The summer devours him vehemently
Arrival of spring is a nightmare to him
Only autumn gives him a hope in Coventry.

When these four are one, all four becomes one.
He becomes a moment's toast!

Young man, rumours have it that,
The WORLD will meet at your *feet*!
Where are your specs to hide your face?
From the cameras of third world nations?
Your senator, that fat bellied husky man,
A dutifully misfit domestic secretary,
Wants you to relocate away from here.
He wants no query,
At the UN general meeting next week.

Call me by Eli,
Your social justice journalist for the moment.
I am one of your own kinds.

The Tot

The bars are left ajar;
The habitués cross-examine the stench.
I thought of a tort
To criminalize one stupid liquid
Which whips wits out of men.
In tots, this thought of tort talked.
I toiled to tow it thoughtfully.
I belong to the Bar Association.
My domestic table, thrice a day, bears three weights,
All courtesy of the Bar Association.
How then shall the sentence be?
Of a bar at the Bar —
Who shall the guilty party be:
The judge, the licensor, the proprietor, or myself?
At the close of a stale day,
We sit ourselves betwixt tables and chairs
With plain and coloured liquids;
In glossy and classy glasses;
Under faint and weak lighting;
With profane and professional songs;
We tilt, whirl, and sway away our worries,
Under the influence of spirits.
This spirit is Smirnoff,
That one is San Simon,
The other one is brandy,
Those are tequilas and whiskeys,
Here is Mandingo.
All are but one spirit,
Doing unto us the same harm,
Both body and soul.

Let the wives who hatch trouble for their husbands
Measure out this harm, both body and soul.

My Black Colonel

He rose like an Arabian spring,
Watering his deprived country to flourish.
His speeches sprinkled the trees of Africa!
What a God's duplicate!
A proud North African god!

Thorny became his life
To a people many Wests away.
For the same fate,
the garment of the old Christ was remembered.
Crucify Him! Crucify Him! Crucify Him!
His own people were bribed and stirred
Until his blood was fervently demanded
when the robe of the old Christ upon his loin fell.

Quickly and noisily the executioners arrived.
In navigable abattoirs they came,
Abattoirs rolled by the new Arab spring.
They caught him
And slaughtered him
On his own African soil.
And a toothless, stupid, and cowardly AU
Boldly did the autopsy.
There he lies.
He is indeed, and in death, our own Gaddafi.
The useless AU shamelessly reported.

Shakespeare

Tremble not thy lips.
Even his associates adored him as the moon.
He favours excellence over glory.
Endless are admiration for him.
He shakes the lexis with his pen
And only the finest words he did spear.
Like a spear,
His plays penetrated multiple languages.
Many a learned scholars still study him today.

Oh my Shakespeare!
Did thou take Hamlet for thy habitat?
That thy where about somehow became unknown?
Or did thou dwelt thyself as Othello?
Lest I comb for thy ghost!
Who made from thy head a Tragedy of Julius Caesar?
Speak unto me his name!
For retribution's account,
I will bid him a visit by the Merchant of Venice.

As You Like It,
May thy Much Ado About Nothing attitude prevail.
Lest, Timon of Athens becomes of you.
I do today tell thy tale as The Winter's Tale
The Sonnets for The Fair Youth
Shall remake the Romeo and Juliet theme.
Thou livest thyself in an All's Well That Ends Well world,
While King Lear, thirsts for a replay of The Tempest.

The Two Noble Kinsmen of which I am one,
Send you a belated birthday pleasantries.

By the hands of The Two Gentlemen of Verona
Shall it be delivered?
Measure for measure, I have a scale place on thy works.
None I lost about Lover's Labour Lost though.
If thy Midsummer Night's Dream be true,
Then must thine ears hear this;
The Twelfth Night of the Taming of the Shrew
Is now The Comedy of Errors.

Has The Merry Wives of Windsor,
made Macbeth anew?
Titus Andronicus and Troilus and Cressida are LOST.
I today celebrate your penmanship.
Let me return to my sturdy,
With versus of Venus and Adonis well read to slumber!

My Legal Prayer

Thou art the most faithful Judge.
Guide my thoughts with ancient wisdom
And my discernment with eternal accuracy.
Equip my tongue with knowledge of equity.
In my court are both the oppressed and the oppressor;
Assist my gavel that it may fall fairly well
On sentences right and just.
Awaken my intelligence within,
That my emotions shall not override my logic.
Preserve in me purity,
That bribery may not soil my gown.
Let me each passing day remember my vows
And oaths to keep.
In my bid to keep justice fair,
Let me not grow poor,
Lest I taint my work with subversions.

Oh Almighty God,
Make me a deliverer of the oppressed,
And a true Justice of the Peace.
Guard my heart that it may not grow greedy.
Tame my thirst for luxury,
Lest I place a tag on my throne.
In my court today,
Lies both the oppressed and his oppressors;
Help me to uncover evidences of oppression intelligently.
In my court today,
Lies the model citizen and the transgressor;
In You alone do I entrust my mental faculty.
Assist me to uncover instruments of wrongdoing.
In my court today,

Lies appellants and their appeals,
Constitutional challenges,
And questions of the law and evidence.
Furnish me with divine wisdom,
That my verdicts may surpass that of others.
And in perpetuity may my wisdom
Be preserved for the benefit of all mankind.
Let me not appear as a parcel of blockhead to posterity.
In You, and all in You,
I pray to draw my discretion.
Give me clues when everyone is clueless;
Arm me with insight when everyone is sightless;
Encourage me when everyone is discouraged;
Help me to prove where everything seems proofless;
And where there are planted proofs,
Help me to disprove logically.
Sanctify my Judgement seat,
That only good judgement may stem from it.
In You I entrust myself this very Day,
Oh Ancient JUDGE.

Iron Soup Villa

Raised on the outskirts of our town,
An exclusive place it is for us.
Shielding us from gossiping eyes and mouths.
It is here we come to feast our hunger away,
With bowlful of foods without protein
accompaniments mounted before us.

And our money is never quite enough to pay.
"Don't worry, sirs, I'll take care of you."
In this manner,
The proprietor manages our hunger.
She knows well how hard money comes by,
Hardly finding its way into our poor pockets;
In our sinking and cash-fevered economy!

Half-Caste

Like a cast
of a medallist,
Like a caste, a seer's caste,
A forge of foul,
A telling of strata's class;
This one was half-cast
According to a certain Castor's caste,
Cast by two unfortunate propagators.

He is now in my already lean and bony country,
Hoping to be picked up and nursed on fertile soil.
Nursed then nurtured,
Nurtured then nursed,
Or both with equity;
on humanitarian grounds.

With his delicate white skin baking **beside** the highways,
My dusty asphalt roads swallow his social vices.
He begs an illusive living,
from the shoulders of the rickety table
of my dying economy.
Felonies of the West!

Mile Sixty

The days of a hired labourer are a long-awaited torpedo toppling to shore.
Serving here, serving there,
Thralldom serves saved purses.
The days of a hired labourer!

Christened dedicated staff,
Fashioned only for hibernation!
On solid-rock sofas a day's beat paused
Who knows our slave master?
Is a black ghost more real than him?

Tell it to me, Mr. Janitor, the office of our employer.
The orifice of a haggler must I assume.
Vigorously, vicariously will I negotiate.
A negotiator's pen I shall gladly mount.

Show us the PRO's domicile,
And locate for us the habitat of the Secretary.
Placards conjugated with stones
Would rainfall be equaled on her roof?

We returned home today,
Without the diamond pod of our sweats.
The earth will grind and chew our boss today.
The labourers' pay beautified the journey anyway.
Like the proceeds of our productive hands,
The fuel to eternity was abundantly bought.
Proceeds of our productions
Produced the proceeding parade.
What a divine funeral of a deity!

Humans feigning gods!
The potbellied, triple-cheeked,
And cushion-napped boss goes to Mile Sixty.

Show me the ledger.
Our putrid Accountant wishes to edit it.
And our erroneous Secretary, who reads erroneously flawlessly,
Seconded him.
Ah, Accountant!
Numbers do not account on Mile Sixty Day, don't you know?
Mile Sixty will settle it, YOU.

When my days are cheaply spent,
And my grey hair eats the decades away,
When satiated Mile Sixty comes, perhaps exhaustively,
I shall fold the remainder of my wrinkled life,
The neatest way I can.
Probably according to the sire's rules, I shall.
Chosen from the big black book, I shall.
And taught from the rostrums of religions, I shall.
To my creator hand it over, I shall.

Expectantly, I shall await his remarks of me,
In the soils once crashed
By the soles of shiny leather shoes of my youth.
The days of a hired man,
Woefully end someday.

Long Solar Eclipse

Gathered on a hill now sit sparks of grey
Bridges bridge not the valleys
Bona fide ban can afford much of nothing
An element of scarcity is what you are now
Who looks for you among the living?
Ownership of self is a free rest
With children who can afford it
How much poverty do you have for sale?
Market night is today!
How much can your mat
Be gifted to a potential buyer?
Psychiatrists do not prescribe groceries!

Gowns make noise
Gavels make noise
Your son's aspiration!
Your nutrition factory is now
A bed for the town's trash
What act of capital offense
Have your simple hands committed?
Perfumes of pungent smell sweeten the aroma!
The caped officer, a garnished moderator, is he today.

Your life serves servitude
Dedicated servant of the law!
No gavel
No cry
No gavel
No cry
The mines you scoop are your graves
Get well, sir!

Injustice pries
Injustice injures
Injuries caused by injustice justices.

Bills talk, sir!
Your seventy-eighth birthday awaits you
The children's mother arranged this jamboree
Her last message, it should be perhaps to you
Check your clock, sir!
Mine reads three decades past a sentence,
And a year past the forget-me-not tree
In an eastern corner somewhere,
Lie the remains of an engagement ring
She wished to observe, rather,
The derelict anniversaries of the matrimony
That she has put up with since your jaildom.

You are a dove
But only sand in a glass can surely say
Time.

Standing Next to History

We will die anyway.
But our acts shall endure longer than we have lived.
Be it good on this side,
Bad on the other side,
The immortal feats achieved by our existence,
Emanate from the generous archives of history.
Men pen it,
Time dates it,
Memory recounts them.
Our perspectives shade our judgement of them.

When denied our rights,
The sleeping beasts within us awake!
Divinity bestowed upon man to freely live.
However, in great esteem man clasps socialisation.
We were therefore made,
To live as individual strands but collectively.
Whenceforth, neighbourship and association became
An inevitable aspect of our lives.
Living as collective strands
On the currency of theories and schemes.
Schemes scheduled by so-called experts.
For the benefit of all it was urged to be.
Then rose giant civilisations:
The Pyramids of Egypt,
The Hanging Gardens of Babylon,
The Statue of Zeus,
The Temple of Artemis,
The Mausoleum of Halicarnassus,
The Colosseums of Rome,
And the Aqueduct of Segovia.

All hailed and praised;
But raised on the backs and shoulders of oppressed men.

So,
In the name of greed, supremacy, and rulers,
Men woke up at moonless dawns to oppress their own kind.
The earth from which we were framed,
Thereupon drank our river of life to inebriation.
Great and paramount was the earth's alimentary canal,
So the flesh, the bones, and the organs
Of nobles and commons, young and old;
It did consume fully to the nourishment of itself.

Hmm.

The forgers forged the swords,
Smiths prepared the shields,
Up went the hollow mouths of cannons,
And catapults towered the fields.
Moderators said their prayers,
Popes recited their Latin chants,
And soldiers wore their prideful armours.
Human beasts thus descended on humanity!
Great were the numbers that
Knelt,
Fell,
And died.

What constitutional right?
What international right?
What universal right?
What human right?
What divine right?

What moral right,
What legal right,
Have you?
Oh Italy!
Oh Spain!
Oh China!
Oh France!
Oh Britain!
Oh Russia!
Oh America!

To tell and determine,
How each free man ought to be governed
In his little country?
When in your hands lie muddy rivers of blood.
Blood of innocent and just people,
To whom your system of governance was preached
With war cries, embargoes, and bombs!

I stand next to history today.
In remembrance of people;
A people whose lives you terminated
Simply on difference of accord.
In memory of Nkrumah,
In memory of Ghaddafi,
In memory of Sankara,
In memory of Luther,
In memory of our destabilised Pan-African continent.
We will all die anyway,
But let each man die naturally.

Quietus' Call

The Sun Is a Jealous Star.
It Is Envious of the Lives Earthlings Live.
In Its Heart Beats Hatred for Man.
Setting Out Each Morning with Wanderlust,
It Burns Man to Wrinkles.
An Umbrella of Consuming Conflagration
Is What It Arcs Over the Fragile Heads of Mortals.

So Are We Gathered Here Today
With Our Bodies Garnished with Cotton, Silk, and Perfume.
So We Forget Our Inevitable Ends.
And Away, and Always,
We Live the Remainders of Our Lives Carelessly.
There's No Time for Repentance,
When Upon an Unknown Day We Are Fed
To Our Nano Homes;
With Wreaths Laid Atop, for Ceiling's Sake.

The Sun Does Count and Number Our Days.
No Act of Dementia Ever Occurred in Its Records.
So It Will Come to Pass, Quietly, Quickly,
That We Will Belong There,
Just the Day After Today,
Or the One Next to It.
We Shall Be Abandoned in the Memorial Groves.
We Shall Be Homed Among Trees Labeled Forget-Me-Not.
There Shall One Stay
To Account for His Actions All Alone.
Even Those Taken in Groups of Friends
Shall Be Answered Solitarily.

A Memorial Stone Shall Stand Erect in Our Place.
The Houses We Built with Sleek Ornaments
Shall Be Swapped for Us.
In Stapled Apartments of Dyed Woods,
We Shall Find Ourselves.
The Farthest Point to Come By,
By Our Loved Ones, Shall Consist of Our Sepulchres.
That Far They Can Go, Never Beyond It.

We May Plan to Live for a Tenfold Decade.
But Our Expirations Come Somewhat Suddenly.
And Away We Go.
What Can Life Amount to Upon Quietus Call?
Nobles and Plebeians,
Kings and Ignoble Citizens,
Corporality Shall Yield Us All to the Other.
"You Do Not Belong Here Anymore," It Says to Man.
Therefore, Man Shall Live,
But Mortally Once.

So While Breath Resides in Our Lungs,
Let Each Man Consult His Maker.
Farewell, Our Dear Beloveds.
Your Remains Shall Not Be Left in A Deserted Grove.
We Shall Save Them in Our Hearts and Immortal Minds.

So Will Our Days Ebb Away
Like the Days of the Many
Who Had Gone On Before Us.
And Our Remains Shall Be Left in Groves,
Where They Shall Give Off Nutrients
To the Very Components
From Which Each Man Derived Existence.

Dust Thus We Are.
And Death's Dust Shall Be Thrown Over Us.
Again, We Will Return to Our Original Place.
Farewell, Oh Our Dear Beloved.
We Shall Come Someday.

Feast of the Vultures

Spread far and wide,
Alpha's sheet became the dinner napkin.
Curved backs of taxpayers
Kept these dinner tables aright.
Labour union leaders folded themselves
For the state's sake,
Then,
The vultures invited themselves,
And their friends,
And on our backs,
They feasted on our country's wealth.
Security forces waited the waiters' waiting,
Serving each one of the scavengers
Enough national resources!

Gates to Sheol

I Saw, when I looked within
Laid atop each other without consent
Under the hot climates of Scandinavia
They know not, nor **see** their neighbours
Yet on this chosen day;
In reverence to their fate they must belong together.

They must abide in these cold chambers
Until the appointed time of segregation
Each shall be parcelled with designer envelopes
Each one shall be mailed to the Creator without prompt.
Jesus and his Antichrist,
Shall upon receipt of the mails,
Statistically and empirically dissociate them
According to Righteousness Law 101,
Grouping them into tribes of predated fates.

No Bullet No Exit

He is half a man, half a bot.
His phalanges bear the likeness of a lion's.
Except **for** my once upon a time dinner with him,
At an all-lights-out retreat,
With all guards on guard,
My knowledge of him is vague and faint.
The media loves his wave,
The banks, his waiver,
But I dread him.
Private things must remain private.
It was under this guise
That we enthroned a leech-buttocked president.
With his glued buttocks,
His adhesive carpus and metacarpus,
And his magnetic cling on power,
Who will dare extract power out of his grip?
No bullet, no exit!

Cathedrals of Same-Lovers

Built on the ashes of Sodom,
With bricks baked and shipped from Gomorrah.
These are the cathedrals for same-lovers.
Cathedrals built for a diabolical agenda.
Coached pastors and priests blessed the marriages.
Farewell to the united groom and groom!
The wedded couples rejoiced in iniquitous harmony!
The said prayers and blessings entered an ear
But not that of Jehovah's.
The couples received answers to their prayers
But not from Christ's lips.

Against them, he wrote;
Mene Mene Tekel Hashmada
Your days are now without infinity.
Destruction has been penned against you.
Cathedrals of same-lovers,
Laid on the rocks of Sodom,
And built with rubble from old Gomorrah.
These are the cathedrals for same-lovers.
Mene Mene Tekel Hashmada!

The Smuggling Parliament

His food consists of only lentils, and more lentils.
He isn't a regular occupant of a lazy bed.
He is a first-class graduate of a certain university.
But he now farms away his engineering knowledge,
on his grandfather's impotent and stony land.
He and his friends live by measure and metre.
They are represented by smuggling MPs.
His MP sits at the far right of an unconcerned Speaker
who orders the house authoritatively
on issues regarding Article 71.

His shout 'ORDER' thunders through the oversized hall
built by a visionary architect
who foresaw the sizes of their bellies.
He sweeps swiftly important documents from the IMF
under his elephant desk,
with an excuse of "time is far spent on the issue."
By this trick, he smuggles away from the nation,
money worth a kingdom's gift!
What a smuggling Speaker for a smuggling Parliament!

I landed my iron feet
on the soft and sofa-smuggling Parliament floor.
I hope to avert matters by becoming an MP.
But I am sworn into office with an oathless paper.
Are labial words alone enough? I asked.
"Do as the Clerk says,"
Mr. Speaker ordered me with an owl's look.

I will take no weightless oath!
I shall resign immediately.

But I am coming back;
to this smuggling Parliament someday,
not by pen nor thumb,
but by the enemy of the ballot.

The Speculative Philosopher

Ko ko ko kokokokooo
Ti ti ti titititiii
Tiko ko tiko ti koko
Ti ti ko ko kokoko ti

My grandfather is a speculative philosopher.
He can tell both the forward and the backward
of a clock from the present.
He tells it by beads, bones, and cowries.
By metal coin, he can too.
A magistrate of our town he is.
From his lips issues both a blessing's goodwill and its woe.
Town folks worship his feet obediently.
A speculative philosopher!

Míawoe nye agbo yee
Míawoe nye agbo yee
Míawoe nye agbo ma'todzo
Míawoe nye agbo gāgawo
Míawoe nye agbo yee
Míawoe nye agbo yee
Míawoe nye agbo ma'ɖuawo
Míawoe nye agbo gāgawo

For the needs of so many wives;
Must he beat his fingers to reflect,
and fulfil each morning's conversation.
Chats on cloth, food, and money
guide his discrete discretions.
And according to such and such needs,
Must he look into the magnetized sacred pots.

And he does it so philosophically.
What a speculative philosopher!

Nane le kɔ me loo
Azizā le kɔ me loo
Nane le kɔ me loo
Azizā le kɔ me loo
Nane le kɔ me ne do va mí do go
Azizā le kɔ me ne do va mí do go
Nane le kɔ me ne do va mí do go
Azizā le kɔ me ne do va mí do go

By toil day and night,
Each client must find enough wealth
To satisfy the tummies of the unknown gods;
To have their misfortunes remedied.
Well-known god.
After all, he is one,
at least now that he is alive.

His wife bloats as she strolls down the town's streets.
Black and grey heads alike
give her the Roman Catholic bow.
The shrine holds for them,
a money-vomiting machine.
A speculative philosopher's federal reserve!
Adela da tu 'me wu akpagba oo
'Kpagba wu gbe yee
'Kpagba wu gbe loo
'Kpagba wu gbe zā la do

On an ancient mat of animal hide,
He spreads his family's needs.

Letting out the beads from crafty fingers.
The cowries dance according to predetermined fates.
When the news is positive,
Fortunes find their way to the shrine, to our traditional depot.
Otherwise ,
Fattened rams and fowls add weight to the kitchen pots.
Grandma's addictive steps frequent the kitchen.

He counts on the client's ignorance and phobias.
The brave get beaten by the mention of the gods' wrath.
Anyway, I have kwashiorkor to cure.
So let me eat those sacred meats till my teeth are white.
It is my lot.
The gods know I diligently sweep their pungent house.
I know them from within.
I come from a family of philosophers.
My grandfather is a traditional philosopher.
But I am a scientific philosopher.

The Image of God

"I will today paint God," said the artist to his student.
"In what colour would the portrait be?" queried the student.
"You know of course! A whole lot of white and some little black!"
"Impressive!" exclaimed the student.
"But why the mixture of black and white?" asked the student.
"Well, well, well, first to avoid street brawls,
And to represent him as the scriptures said," answered the master.
"Which scriptures, sir?" inquired the student.
The art master replied: "Christian scripture, which said through him all things were made."
"Including good and evil?" the boy asked.
"From the premise, yes!" answered the artist.
"Isn't he supposed to be kind and merciful?" he again asked.
"Only to his chosen ones," opined the artist.
"He created all but chose only a few?" asked the student.
In reply, the artist said:
"For the act of one man he chose the Jews.
For the life of another man, he again chose some."
"Isn't that partiality?" interrogated the boy.
"Well, you may be right," the artist replied.
"If he created us all, why are we of different skin colours?" demanded the boy.
"Well, my little boy, God is of different shades;
In such shades he made man," said the artist.
"To some, he torments people in hell,
To others, he is just and righteous.
Some see him as a God of war,
Others see him as a rightful avenger.
The good thing is, we can make him in whatever image we wish.

Come on, boy!
Let us paint God in our own image."

Eliana

Tonight, I will again complete a circuit.
A circuit of seven uncountable nights of insomnia.
I am a farmer of sleep myself.
But of late, I have not a single drop of sleep in my barrels.
The desert has more riches of water than my barrels!

I have four rounds of four guards.
Stationed cardinally in fours in my domicile, they are.
Like a commando, they are well-trained and armed.
What can dare a thief to enter my habitat?
Yet, a harmless thief took the challenge.
A thief has stolen into the secret place of my privacy.

The battle of defence I have mercilessly lost.
My thoughts stare at me aghast!
My nights are garnished
With her aesthetic beauty,
Yet, I never seem to have enough.
What medicine did lovicians prescribe for lovesickness?

I have fallen in love with a demi-goddess!
A feminist superior of all.
I once wrestled her and shamefully got beaten.
I again contended with her the other day, and we both lost.
I am fighting her again, can you guess the result?

On the altar of bonds,
I have found something — my heart!
The thief took my heart to the altar of bonds.
Eliana has left my heart and its passions on an altar.
Love is the divine parson at this temple.

I long ago settled my differences with love
During the dinner of nobles — passions.

My exchequer court passed a bill last night,
When I, upon the Judicial Chair, briefed my woes.
But he comprehended me not.
I summoned the Chief Security,
As an ancient guest listener to my woes.
Yet he lacked understanding in the matter.
My abled security marshals,
He moved to declare redundant!
Matters of the heart are not comprehension passages,
Neither do they avail for judicial interpretations.

I remember not the last time
I siphoned mother's breast.
Yet, in the chest of Eliana,
I smelled mother's aura;
The bond that connects us
Across many miles and time.

Switch off public access tonight!
Lower lowly low the domicile flag.
Close the reception desk.
Circulate to visitors my absence of presence.
I will have Eliana in my chamber tonight.
I will converse with her in distilled silence.
Only shadows moulded by moonlight can be our witness,
A cast against an immortal wall,
That tells a perpetual history of us,
Cast in diamond, written in stars.

Cross over the hills and mountains of difference,
And meet me in the valley of love, my paramour!
My dear inamorata,
Don't give your ears to diffusive deceitful speech,
Lest they truncate our joyous destiny.
Demi-god and goddess we are among mortal men.
Let our immortality's reign rain in an unabridged love.
For myriads of years,
I will make impervious our love.

Come down to the river of affection,
Where the waters water our passions.
Let us bathe, this way and that way,
In the warmth of love till eternity calls.

My room sits in the uppermost precinct of that storey.
I love mauve, gold, red and white.
I have an amaranthine love for incense and perfumes.
So I gave my room these flavours.
I love to see the lights twerk and twinkle in my room.
I love to hear the sound bar
Dose the air with country and cool music.
Play the likes of Williams, Dion, Dolly and Bryan.

Accept me today.
I need to have milligrams of sleep.
The clock speaks of the first hour of dawn to me now.
But here I am,
In the bud of love meditations.
Insomnia has gotten the best of me.
Look into my eyes, Eliana!
There is where I left the insignia for you.
I will love you in the morning.

At noon, I will not hate you.
In the eventide, I shall bring you into covenant;
With red and violet background.

Dear Eliana, this is the issue with me.
Help me make sense of my passion.
It is a matter of the heart!
I am retracting my footsteps to my hermit.
There is where I will belong,
In pure isolation, until I hear from your lips.
Eliana!

My Assassination

Sandwiched between verges of my garden,
There they stood,
Bearing a letter written in red dye,
Beneath which lay my signature.
My trusted secretary outwitted me;
Here I stood, condemned by my own signature.
To seal his aim, a pistol hung conspicuously.
Here stood I, shoulder to shoulder with an assassin,
On fresh garden soil I tilled just yesterday.
Here I stood on my own toil with a man,
Who until yesterday was enrolled on my payroll,
Breathing a frog's breath with no conscience.
I was made to dig a grave comfortable enough
For my future body yet unvarnished.
Is our national flag red, gold and green?
If so, I must have been wrapped well,
Buried in bright national colours like a statesman.
My assassination came so politically politely.

The National Cathedral

We pledged and promised on our honours
To remain faithful and loyal;
To a nation at the centre of the earth.
But our leaders pledged likewise unto their stomachs.
We are a nation, though,
but not a divine one.

However, they came to heap up a structure.
A structure of corrupt sand and cement.
They built a modern pyramid with taxpayers' money.
True and dignified ones, with cassocks of impunity,
came to dedicate it to our unknown national God.
By several banknotes, this structure went up,
while the people die bedless in hospitals.
Does God hear prayers
from responsibility-shirking leaders?

They call it The National Cathedral.
A cathedral for Christians' Christ,
A cathedral for Jews' Jehovah,
A cathedral for Muslims' Muhammad,
A cathedral built by appalling leaders,
with Christian trade names!

Exile

After our homes got destroyed by metal rains,
After our politicians stole the nation's wealth,
After darkness captured our schools,
After we were betrayed by our own parents,
After we became unemployed upon leaving school,
After they sold our resourceful lands into slavery,
After they forced and passed unworthy bills,
After we paid monies they borrowed for their spouses,
After they repelled our demonstrations with the deadliest ammo,
After they bestowed infinite reign upon themselves,
After they openly discarded our basic needs of life,
After crimes became 'pay as you go' for the affluent,
After corruption was seconded by our chief whips,
After they openly told us power would never leave their claws,
After they corrupted the military and turned them upon us,
After they used terrorism for their own benefit,
After institutions committed crimes they were built to fight,
And after our constitution was willingly discarded,

All our dreams, hopes, and visions went into exile.

V-Day

It marks a day of a hobby.
A day of valency!
Intelligent atoms pair
their outermost and innermost electrons on this day.
In rooms of shuttered lights,
sealed doors and opaque curtains,
they pair well.
Levonorgestrels will carry out
the emergency cleansing exercises with purity,
erasing participants' mess with excellence.
This eraser will secure for all innocent participants
a certificate of non-participation.
An insurance against disgrace!
What a divine eraser!
Leaving no trace nor trail of any pairing.
It is not in vain that we clad this day in red.
On this day, evil befalls many.
And the grand generosity of many parties
pays off well.

Black Friday

I saw from offshore
How giant howling canoes, migrating them, came.
They came with a windy force.
And we had to send them back with triple the force!
An absolute disobedience to Newton's Law.

On days like this,
After Thanksgiving Thursday,
Masters get swapped at depreciated values.
These painters painted black the Friday,
With their ebony skins.
From long halls of howls beneath white feet,
they came.

From offshore,
I saw giant whales with sailing backs;
Meandering their routes towards our filthy soils.
Upon arrival, they filled our tanks with tequila,
Making brains burn from inebriation.
Oh, their civilisation's souvenirs dazzled us.

They built fortified forts and cast castles.
We saw castellated cells beneath their free feet
Only to realise our fares were paid in kind!
Too late, we were deceived! one chief cried out.
You were deceived indeed and in deeds!
After all, alcoholised brains do not reason.

Our kinds were housed beneath their soles.
And the later generations of Africans
Chose to forever remain footstools.

Begging alms here and there
For survival in their mismanaged economies!
Our kinds were packaged for a forever trip.
The labelled dungeons paved way for a Friday
Which is Black.

Restitution

I don't mingle my mind's mine with mental slaves.
I inform to formally reform for transformation.
Formal reformation fights fearlessly forward.
I separate to subtract myself
From a communal, communicable contamination.

Restitute our destitute institutes constitutionally.
You teach teachers teaching,
But hate Hare's call to teach politicians patriotism.
You prefer practices of pilfering in politics.
Importing decomposed democracies degradingly derails our nation.

I pray prayerfully,
To regress gracefully our polluted politicians' policies.
I police the police of our poor country.
To be one, one needs a tribal affidavit–protocol passport!
Nepotism neglects nationalism.

Keep our economy immaculate,
And immunise it against monetary mortality.
Dollars don't die.
Why extract cedis from our emaciated poor pockets?

IMF betrayed BoG through fiscal fissures,
Devaluing values of our currency,
To corrode our current currency cuts necks.
Promulgate promotional policies to promote our products.
Holy Host, hold our hanging nation.

Divert this controversial course!
No connection contracts communists
To socially sorted socialists.
Dear police,
Politely poison these political prostitutes.
Mr Speaker,
Speak to the Special Prosecutor,
To restitute the nation for unlawful monetary masturbation.

Like a bygone I will be gone,
But my gong will never be gone like a war wagon.
Restitute the country for the financial lobotomisation
Caused by organised political criminals.

Restitute our passive social institutions,
But build no such buildings like auxiliary agencies.
Efficacy disdains duty duplications,
So stop the political interferences;
A high treason under Law of National Progress it is.

How do we punish criminals
Who make crimes for us,
For committing crimes they did not make for themselves?
I rest to wrestle.

The Ancient Thief

A thief was he,
when he departed from his father's house.
Within the endless bosom of the wilderness,
his tired and worn-out soul thirsted for a rest.
On a cold ground of weeds and a rock as a headrest,
he passed the night.

Since the stolen fortune was not gold nor silver,
the robber who attempted to steal;
upon hearing of this thief's great treasure,
found for himself nothing except a wrestle.
An affidavit was sworn thereof,
and the old ID gained erasure.

The old thief stood with a new ID.
A pass to Laban's house was thus gained.

Decades became the years;
yet low was the stolen fortune's growth.
Ancient thief as he was, he took to artifice,
and his master's livestock he recoloured.

Since by theft a living he made,
it served him right when a thief was made his wife.
Cursed became his wife for a theft abominable,
but the old thief blossomed.

And we remembered how angels visited him
on the night of rest in the wilderness.
And he procreated a mighty nation.
This old thief made for us a Saviour's birthplace.

Asylum Down

He lives down that street.
By law and genetics, he may be a father to me.
A dweller of House No. 4AS, built by yours truly with invisible bricks.
Having no co-tenant, he rests, feels at ease, and free.
He lives in an asylum,
On the far end of Mental Asylum Street.
A victim of divorce!

Hotel Laliga

I come here each summer.
To shed my skin anew.
This Hotel was built with exquisite skills.
Perfectly
Hanging
On
The
Moon
And,
Resting
As well
On
Land.

Night Always blends me the usual smoothies
Even After satiation from many devoured flesh,
Night Makes sure I belch.

Each Bed bearing weights of two,
Knows the blenders.
The Night does not delay
Bringing in the mixed sounds of pleasures and regrets.
Condolences To the unlucky ones
Who expire from suffocation,
Of massive meats they dare to eat!

Only I, breaks the rule of two here.
I am forbidden from the lavish section.
I will be going again this year.
But not again as a Laliga spectator

I Will play as well.

I May.

Hollow Cathedral

They look good from outside.
On Rich Avenue their memories stay.
Memories of once existent labours
Of once-upon-a-time dreamt visions.
Their glamour was dictated by architects,
And painstakingly ironed into each block.
Much less of it may be adored today.

Admirable things and rust are not affable friends.
If you think you can tell:
At sixty, youth nostalgia rusts your retirement.
At fifteen, you want it fast.
At twenty, you hop onto the fast-track train.
At thirty, the barrister's office becomes your library.
At forty, the bank prints you a life summary.
Life indeed begins at forty!

How much did you spend at the parenthood supermarket?
At the marriage mart?
Hollow Cathedral,
Weeds settle on the roofs to announce their dejection!

Psalm 151

Oh Yahweh! In you alone we thrust our trust!
What is man to you?
It is four less than a week's eggs,
Since the official sacrificial lamb was slaughtered.
His appointed ones acted out the betrayal and denial.
And the Romans did the slaughtering for us.
But permanently high have you lifted our errors.
The transgressions of our lives partitioned us from you.
You broadcasted our prayers on iron soils.
But you alone have I known by name and colour.
Your wills dwell many a page down history's white books.
Aba! Aba!
Freely flow forth,
From Zion, fountains of pity!
Season our stale lives with joys,
And rest peacefully our souls.
Let every flesh retire in harmony.
Because troubled have our days been according to your wrath,
And our nights shivered in pains!
Just Jah, just be thy justice.

Ambush

Lay low, loyal brothers!
Lay flat, sincere sisters!
The journey on which we set our minds is long.
The path upon which we establish our treads is wavy.
A long path for our short lives!

The freedom fighters who opened paths for us are no more.
The seasoned leaders with wisdom are gone.
The patriotic ones who saluted us on our way to school are dead.
Jubilees ago, our future resided with us.
But China now owns it!

Crawl until you are steady, brother.
Toddle until you can run, sister.
Then and there, we can run all by ourselves.
We have been betrayed.
Betrayed by our own parents, we are.
We are ambushed by our own people.

Let this tale of ours be told after we are gone.
To the generations that will stem from us, let it.
Tales of our toils and of our strength's products,
Which poured into the hollow purses of our nation's architects.
They craft for us contingencies and crimes.
But for themselves,
they built forts **of** immunities and privileges.

We have been ambushed!
Brother, sister, let us learn to think.
Let us think outside a subjugated mind.
And stop living in borrowed souls.

Let us search the mountains and deserts
For lost scrolls of wisdom.
Inside the deepest depths must we dip our tiny arms
To dig out the lost maps of our minds.
Our freedom will be birthed by our searches;
Freedom from mental hegemony!

They have ambushed us educationally.
But onwards must we prevail,
redeeming our lives from the entanglement.
From the cruel manacles of our parents, let us break free.

Look on this side of the road, sister.
Watch the opposite, brother.
Let me guard the back.
Together, we must watch our future.
Lest they steal it from us.
We have been ambushed!
A giant snare has trapped us
On the road to our future.
We have been ambushed!

The Evils of Our Professions

He is a first-class product of our enviable university.
The topography of sapiens is accurately engraved on his brain.
With exceptional skills,
He butchers and sews his own kinds.
His office is the one where furious ambulances
Vomit half-caught victims of death into.
By his licensed needles,
Lethal substances run down our veins with liberty;
With an adduced docket,
He dissociates our lungs and hearts from us.
Aye, many a young man aspires to be like him.
He titles himself Immigration Officer.
And the nation trusts him for it.
He is a known imported immigrant.
But he sits himself at our ports and borders,
In ported and bordered cubicles!
At his beck, many a piece of luggage is bisected and inspected
In search of evidence of premeditated ingredients of crime.
Yet, with similar nods, the white powder for our noses remains unchecked.
He titles himself an Immigration Officer,
And the nation trusts him for it.
The vile nature of our professions!

His skull is void.
Whether right or wrong, he cannot decipher.
He is a certified lethal equipment operator.
A duty he does well.
He meets cold unionists who demonstrate
At 5:45 GMT, he reverberates the firing range with his AK-47 'death',

Claiming the lives of criminals of equal credentials
As our politicians whom he protects.
Yet, he safeguards the thieves of our state so professionally.
His skull lacks ether profoundly.

She garnishes herself in a long white overall.
Her office sits within the premises of abbreviations.
She has the entire USP and BP inscribed on her brain for good.
A meticulous moderator of medicaments!
She is the mechanic I visit on body maintenance days.
She checks me in with organized, summarised smiles.
The young women of my town,
Who wish to hang their pregnancies,
In order to be virgins anew;
Get their mifepristone and misoprostol from her.
Killer of unborn neonates!
The evils of our professions!

He's a nocturnal soul.
His residency lies behind the Police flats.
We scarcely see him, much less hear him.
By his title, CID Boss, are we to identify him.
His guilty eyes always seek salvation
Behind a twin of sunglasses.
Affixed to his mind are names of opposition figures.
His hands are dyed with the blood of journalists and lawyers.

His office inspires the youth.
By virtue of his work, he is esteemed above town folks.
Black gown or brown gavel, he presides.
His brilliant brain and sharp tongue wash doves in mud and swine to white.
By his pen,

Our church moderator, who modulates our morality on moral modules,
Who spoke against homosexuality,
Was sent to the guillotine.
The vile nature of our professions!

Genesis of the Beginning

Myriads of years ago,
On ages long past, lost and forgotten,
And on the shoulders of antiquity,
Ancients came to be.
Supernaturals they were called.
From a common in situ they emerged.

But chaos often arrests their tranquility.
Who dwells at the apex of superiority?
Who sits in the precincts of command?
These interrogative reasonings bred the altercations.

Since from a known source they all came;
From minute drips of holy matter and many threadlike conjugants,
It chanced upon them to settle an agreement.
To forever sever the troubles,
A competition was enacted.

Some did not see it right
To contest for the sceptre of superiority.
Possessing awareness that impartiality does not fuel hatred,
The few fair ones became Judges.

On that fateful day;
All had arrays of ingenuity for exhibition.
Profoundly gorgeous,
Splendidly exquisite,
And spectacularly awful were the exhibits!
Rewards of approval poured benevolently.

Also, amidst them was Je, son of Hovaah.
This Hovaah procreated them by craft.
With the conjugation of holy matter, he too came into being.
For this logic, it was inscribed;
From the incomplete comes the complete.

Je, master architect, was deemed to be.
He fashioned an expanse,
And spread it wide and far.
He sprinkled burning filaments across the expanse
To furnish it with unmitigated beauty.
He formed numerous elemental specimens,
And had them installed on hovering plates.
He scattered the plates intelligently across the expanse.
This was the grandiose exhibit of Je.

It came to pass,
Je's art surpassed the rest in brilliance!
A victor he became among his contemporaries.
To him also, new titles were given;
Je, The Creator of Galaxies
Je, The Founder of the Universe
Je, The Most Intelligent Creator

The success of Je did not sit right with one of them.
Unpleased, he rivalled Je's handiworks to the hilt!
Envy and jealousy took over the wellness of his thoughts.
So he fashioned destruction,
Which he cast into Je's art in his absence.
Upon Je's awareness of the evil a brother begot,
He set out to amend things.
Since good he ever was and would be,
So it seemed right and just before him to correct all wrongs.

But luck was on the part of some of the creation of JeHovaah,
Yes, the creations of Je, son of Hovaah, understood these matters.
So, by Je's brother's cruelty,
Nature malfunctions to produce disasters.

Elisha Sheindy

Standing erect I am tonight
At the foot of a podium
where religious novels get read,
To the hearing of our forever bottomless ears.
Spiritual digest for two little doves.

The chapel radiated joy,
Which lingered for decades unseen,
Except for the eyes of my stubborn nocturnal neighbour.
To make me sure he saw us last night, he asked,
"Erm, your friend 'Lisha didn't mention hello to me last night.
You sure there's nothing wrong?
Pulsing beats hallowed me.
Said were the vows
Exchanged were the rings and kisses.

Spread your luscious little fingers on my trunk.
Snake up and down
The contour of my thorax.
I will take no valium tonight.
The nectar of thy lips will suffice for sleep for me.

Look at my soul in purity.
I will likewise look at yours.
Let us integrate ourselves on this fair day.
Like nuts fitting tightly in bolts.

I will access your domestic port tonight.
I will taste your meat pie on this night.
Conduct me into your contoured well!
Open wide your biological forceps.

Avail your inns at me
and moan the pleasures away.
Take me by your index and thumb.
Yes, by fingers of marital iniquities!
Tilt this way and that way,
I have hurdles to surmount along this way.
Give me an angle of satiation,
And make me a living piston.

Speak my name in lilts of love.
My ears will decode them.
Wet your flawless body with exotic oils.
Customize your violet gown with foreign fragrance.
Arrange your adorable ebony body in blue.
I shall mount thee tonight!

Your kiss springs streams from my loin.
I have my own milky way,
Will you be its reservoir?
Let me deposit my signature in you.
Let us make new earthlings
according to our beauties.
Make them according to your feminine powers.

Give me a low dose of tonight's moonlight.
Paint my tent with your forever captivating voice.
I cannot compare today's day with any other.
Allow me a ride of adventure
in the darkness of today's eventide.
To a destination of untold adventures, I wish to go.

Grant me an up-down, down-up
swing into your grooved shrine.

Receive me full length without rejection.
Let me feel compressed flesh all around me.
Suffocate me with an unadulterated tightness.
Unconditionally, my love is for you.

Elisha, what if I tell thee a poem?
What if a riddle I do say?
Rest thy head upon my chest this day.

The Great Tree of Life

Standing on the summit,
Of the mountain of Transgression,
Piercing the gloomy skies of separation,
Is the great tree of life!

Planted without soil, yet!
Planted without seeds, no!
Planted without care, yes!

It grew quickly for harvest.
Its bark was struck by sin,
And it revealed a red sap.
From it, mankind's freedom issued.

Nuclear Night in Donbas

From my little cabled window
Of a little windowless office,
I saw an evening's fireworks.
The cracks are heart-stopping.
The sounds, ear-splitting.

In times recently past,
A young man came to be there.
Sitting astride a land so wide,
Mightier than the powers of the West, his nod was.
Great power sat on his young and weak shoulders.

It came to pass,
That his heart led him astray
And his mind misguided his propensity.
So he grew hostile in his old skin.
Waking up on a night's morning,
His generals were summoned to weigh his significance.
For fear of fear,
None dared to refute his order.
A mighty army backed his beck
When his attention rested upon a neighbour.

Like a wounded cat, many tamers fled from his sight,
Abandoning a powerless prey to pray its own prayers.

From my giant window,
Of my celled office room,
I saw the fireworks.
Rest well, oh inhabitants of Donbas!

Civilization

On ages ago, unknown to man,
On the far left of antiquity,
And on an undated day of a certain century,
Man tapped into the sacrosanct of awareness.

Upon the recipient of awareness in a deadly dose,
Man took to subduing nature.
Soon, writing and interpretation arrived
To witness the voguish adventure of man.
Afterwards, civilization was birthed.

Civilization seemed more important to man.
Some thus parcelled and sold theirs;
Their buyers paid dearly for it!
Kings mighty in rulership and great on thrones,
Rose and divided humans, lands, seas, and time,
According to their desired portions.

Bearded men swayed under the waves of each collapsed civilization.
Man crawled from beneath the rubble,
Only to rise again and again,
Dodging the whip of extinction so artfully.
In the arms of survival,
Progenies were hidden from the inevitable.

The earth, however, suffered from the hands of man,
So it called for help.
To remedy this,
Man began a search for God.
The Jews searched and found Yehweh

Behind the arching clouds.
Christians found Christ on the stake of Golgotha,
Buddhists kowtowed to the philosophies of Buddha,
Desert dwellers found Mohamed on the mountain of thirst,
Africans found divine potency in stones and rivers.

Too little did the search prove helpful for man.
Disputes and disparities were settled on the fields of slaughter,
Rather than temples, synagogues, and mosques.
Spears whistled through dust invented by chariots.
Bartering rams breached walls.
The shortfalls of catapults were catered for by cannons.
Bombs winglessly flew,
Wailed and drilled out man from his home.
In mushroom clouds,
The likes of Hiroshima and Nagasaki tasted the bitter sap of extinction.
Today, we welcome technology.
We call it twenty-first-century modernisation.
Born-again Christians are now porn-again.
Prostitution is sanctioned as Slay Queening.
Whores TikToked profanities to the admiration of Christian followers.
And ladies gave out dignity in exchange for eyephones,
All done under the auspices of civilisation.
These are far we have come!

The Pen, the Gun

Mightier than the emperors of old,
Greater than the distinguished Napoleon.

Sharper than the spears of Alexander,
More powerful than the words of Cyrus.

Slim and stiff,
Strong but swift,
It bravely tears a man's motives apart,
Word for word,
Thought for thought.

It evades the oceans of white seas,
It digs up dirt,
And conceals the errors of masters.

A companion to students,
A secretary to clerks.
If pencils be made of the ashes of slaves,
Let the pen of our killers
Be filled with their blood!

Tides

The tides untied themselves.
Behind our sights, we enthroned the dethroned.
We balloted against battling bullets without deciphering
The devil stealthily portrayed himself
Onto our ballot papers.
Our thumbs plonked him discreetly.
And away, we
d
r
o
p
p
e
d
Like graceless grapes into our graves gravely
After the elections.

Prayer of a Faithful Wife

Young I was when I first donned these robes.
Except for a peruke of esquires,
I nearly looked like one.
A new me I begot in clad robe,
and the church bowed to me.
A priest I am destined to be.

The holy thorny carpet of my parish
smelled the pain of her knees.
Tears wet her veil.
The walls repeated her prayers.
Today marks the holiest day of the week.
It marked their nineteenth anniversary too.
I did remember that.
It was their union I blessed
when I first became a priest.
What a holy convocation it was!

Many are the old calendars,
and she became a constant object in my dominion.
Her husband's deeds have kept it as such.
She goes without food for many days.
Empty pantry feeds no plates after all.
Just as her husband,
I equally failed to remedy the problem.

I returned to my wife-less and lonely bed.
But her prayers kept beating at my doors.
"Ooh merciful Father!
Grant the heart of cherubs to my dissociated husband.

Father, for the children's sake, do him no harm.
But let the younger women cast his lips and wallet aside."

Pilgrims

Here we are, with torn soles and ripped heels.
Our weary feet's testimony!
Our feet shredded by dust.
Without an aim, without a bearing,
We arrived as pilgrims on a pilgrimage.

The guardian who forgot our bearing,
Gave us empty charts.
Upon the coldest northern deserts,
On the evergreens of the equator,
On the driest lowlands of the deserts,
He scattered us.
We crept through the lengthy journey,
Without guaranteed necessities.
With pain and rejection,
We journeyed as pilgrims
On a pilgrimage to an unknown end.

Mystery of Creation

Chapter 1

When man was born,
Uncivilised and wanting was the earth found.

Man became hungry,
So he took leaves and meat.
But it did him no good.
Man first took fruits,
And it separated awareness from ignorance,
Wisdom from folly, and good from bad.

According to this wisdom, man harvested the earth,
And named its occupants according to their kinds.
A named day and night passed, thus was day one.
Man went on to craft wood, stone, and metals into domestic and farm tools.
A day's night passed, and it was the second.

Upon learning the art of building dwellings,
Man went out of caves to organise into societies.
A day was swallowed by night, the third day.

On the fourth day, greed overthrew the goodwill of man.
Man conquered and subjugated his own fellows into colonies.

Before a day and a night had passed, man wired one house to another,
The fifth of the days.

On the sixth day, man took rubber, metal, and glass.
With them, he fashioned mechanical beings according to his

image.
Good and bad, he made them.

All that he made looked good and splendid and plausible.
And his heart was glad over them.
He gave unto the metal beings excessive intelligence.
A day and its mother passed, day seven.

On this day, man went extinct.

Freestianity

Exactly four figures ago,
A birth was registered in Asia.
Onto that birth is today marked Xmas.
A saviour saving senior sinners sincerely each day.

It thus occurred to me,
To at least be Nicodemus today.
So I went to a parish,
To have my sins weighed and turned over.

Upon entering,
The engineer who spins the music at my X-Club
Preached unto me Christ's salvation with the piano.
The pole dancer at my gay club translated her voice into heavenly worship.
So I went back home with my truckload of sins.

There is freedom in deed in Christianity.
After all, by betrayal and denial, it was born.

Putting Putin Put

It was just an hour’s past,
But grey and wan has his hair become.
His smiling face was not spared a wrinkle's touch,
Nor has his strength been exempt from fading.
His mighty arms, that once lifted up nations,
Are now but weak and worn.

To reconcile,
He verges his anger to the world.
His demands toppled many a great nation.
But he must go, just as he came,
Whether with a sun's shine,
Or a night's shade,
Put Putin Put.

There Is

There is an acknowledged pat,
And a debilitating riot in Patriotism.

There is a livid demon,
And a scant ration in Demonstration.

There is a legal commerce,
And an invisible death in Soldiering.

There is a straining bell,
And a believable lie in Belief.

There is a notable science of morality,
And a convincing understanding in Conscience.

There is a deterring delay,
And an addictive memory in Determination.

There is a devouring lure,
And a destructive ailment in Failure.

There is a honing verge,
And an instantaneous moment in Knowledge.

There is an entrenched impartiality,
Built on a firm limb, in Legality.

There is a degree of injury,
And a long forearm in Harmony.

In everything and anything,
There is both good and bad.

There Is a Limit

If you can realise that there is a limit on most things in life;
A limit on how much you can give,
A limit on how much you can receive,
A limit on how much you can eat,
A limit on how much you can have,
A limit on how much you can share,
A limit on how long you can live,
A limit on how long you can sleep,
A limit on how long you can repress,
A limit on how long you can be opposed,
A limit on how long you can laugh,
A limit on how long you can weep,
You would be more considerate.

Walk down the street,
Eulogise the achievements of your friends,
Nourish your relationships with praise and gratitude.
Life is a one-way trip,
You will be at this point just once.
Soon, all of today's deeds will wane into memory.
Life is a one-way trip,
Tread with caution.

We Shall Be

The rain will not cease; even if it does,
The fields will not wither; even if they do,
Our livestock shall not perish, even if they do,
Our corrupt governments shall topple, even if they do,
Love shall not become stale, even if it does,
Hunger shall not subdue our lands, even if it does,
Pandemics shall not erase us, even if they try,
Science will not disappoint us, even if it does,
Failure will not deter us, even if it does,
Wickedness will not undo us, even if it does,

We will not forget we are humans.
Forever, we shall be victors.

Mortal Me Immortal

I shall be mortal just once.
Before this life, I was never one.
After this life, I shall never again be one.
What life begat me for, I shall do.
Spirits have lived for countless ages;
To perhaps their perfections attained.
I have only this short while to live a blemished life.

Death is neither superior nor inferior to me.
We are both two great but opposing forces.
Where and when death exists,
I do not exist.
Where and when I exist,
Death does not exist.
Death only wins one phase of the race,
When earthly life betrays me as a mortal earthling.

Mortal me immortal,
I shall be mortal just once.
I was never one before.
And, I shall never again be one.
I shall be mortal just this once.

9 789348 892683

Printed at Repro India Ltd.